MW00331942

THE TEENS' WORKBOOK TO SELF REGULATE

Empowering Teenagers to Handle Emotions With Success through Coping Strategies and CBT Exercises

Richard Bass

© Copyright 2022 - All rights reserved.

The content contained within this book may not be reproduced, duplicated or transmitted without direct written permission from the author or the publisher.

Under no circumstances will any blame or legal responsibility be held against the publisher, or author, for any damages, reparation, or monetary loss due to the information contained within this book, either directly or indirectly.

Legal Notice:

This book is copyright protected. It is only for personal use. You cannot amend, distribute, sell, use, quote or paraphrase any part, or the content within this book, without the consent of the author or publisher.

Disclaimer Notice:

Please note the information contained within this document is for educational and entertainment purposes only. All effort has been executed to present accurate, up to date, reliable, complete information. No warranties of any kind are declared or implied. Readers acknowledge that the author is not engaged in the rendering of legal, financial, medical or professional advice. The content within this book has been derived from various sources. Please consult a licensed professional before attempting any techniques outlined in this book.

By reading this document, the reader agrees that under no circumstances is the author responsible for any losses, direct or indirect, that are incurred as a result of the use of the information contained within this document, including, but not limited to, errors, omissions, or inaccuracies.

2 FREE Bonuses!

Receive a **FREE** Planner for Kids and a copy of the
Positive Discipline Playbook by scanning below!

Contents

Part 2
CBT Behavioral Techniques

Introduction

It takes courage to grow up and become who you really are.

- E.E. Cumings

Did you know that modern teenagers experience similar levels of stress as adults? What's worse, many teens underestimate the physical, mental, and emotional impact that stress has on their well-being.

In a 2017 survey conducted by the American Psychological Association (APA), many teens cited that school-related stress (83%), making it into a good college or deciding what to do after high school (69%), and financial issues at home (65%) were common sources of stress (Smith, 2020).

Another APA survey found that more than half (55%) of young people turn to social media for emotional support. The downside however, is that for 45% of them, social media can trigger feelings of insecurity, and cause them to feel bad about themselves (American Psychological Association, 2018).

While being exposed to healthy levels of stress can enhance task performance, promote critical thinking, and promote emotional development, it is important for growing teens to learn effective stress management skills that will help them regulate strong emotions and thrive under pressure.

Adolescence comes with a number of different physical, emotional, cognitive, and behavioral changes. However, these changes don't have to interfere with your child's learning, mental health, self-image, or relationships.

This workbook has been designed to help pre-teens and teenagers between the ages of 9 and 16, learn how to cope with stress. They will be introduced to a form of behavioral therapy known as CBT, which seeks to increase awareness of negative thoughts and emotions and find healthier coping strategies to handle stress and anxiety.

This particular age group is growing up in a modern society, where they are faced with modern problems affecting different aspects of their lives. The purpose of this workbook is to expose them to coping skills that may not be taught at school, and show them how to gain more control over their emotions and make good decisions.

After going through all 42 exercises, teens will feel empowered to confront life challenges, equipped with their new psychological toolbox, full of useful skills and techniques!

Chapter 1

At-Home Therapy for Teens

> We don't create our feelings; they simply come to us, and we have to accept them. The trick is to welcome them.

- Hector Garcia Puigcerver

Should Teens Get Therapy?

Feeling stressed, having mood swings, or getting in trouble at school are common teenage issues. However, there comes a point when these common issues interfere with your daily life. For example, your anxiety might cause you to dread standing up in front of the class and present a speech, or your negative self-talk might cause you to constantly put yourself down and feel inferior to other people.

Not feeling like your normal self is usually a big warning sign that it is time to get professional help. Speaking to a therapist can help you identify potential mental health issues that are behind some of the physical, emotional, and behavioral changes you are experiencing. The therapist can also teach you coping skills to address ongoing stress and anxiety, so that you can navigate your teenage years successfully.

Therefore, the answer to the question, "Should teens get therapy?" is a resounding yes! But remember that therapy isn't only for people who are "mentally ill." This is a big misconception that tends to make teens avoid seeking support. You don't have to wait until you experience something traumatic, or get diagnosed with a mental health condition to seek therapy. You may simply desire to vent to someone who isn't related to you, who can listen to your thoughts and feelings without judgment.

Therapy From the Comfort of Your Bedroom

You might be the type of teen who prefers to open up to a select number of people whom you trust. The thought of speaking to a therapist may not sound exciting, especially if you have had bad experiences in the past. The good news for you is that therapy doesn't have to involve anyone else but you!

Yes, you can become your own therapist.

Although not much research has been undertaken to explore self-therapy, there is enough evidence to show that self-directed mental health interventions, like reading self-help books, downloading a mental health app, or practicing self-care strategies are effective in improving your overall well-being.

Not only is this method of therapy affordable, it can also help you take responsibility for your own mental health and experiment with skills and strategies that work best for your personality and lifestyle.

This workbook promotes self-therapy, but doesn't rule out the need for seeking professional support.

Its goal is to simply empower you to take control of your health, confront personal challenges at your own pace, and teach yourself psychological tools that will make your life feel more fulfilling.

How CBT Works

The type of psychotherapy that you will learn from this workbook is called cognitive behavioral therapy (CBT). It explores the world of thoughts and emotions, and helps you understand the relationship between what you think and feel and how you behave or relate to others.

One of the main benefits of CBT is its problem-focused approach to dealing with stressful life situations. It seeks to address issues by looking at what you can do right now to alleviate stress and anxiety, and feel stronger to make it through tough times.

Research shows that CBT is an effective intervention to treat mental health issues like anxiety, depression, eating disorders, and substance abuse (Cleveland Clinic, 2022). It can also help you understand and adjust certain behaviors, such as overthinking, social awkwardness, overly criticizing yourself, and easily getting frustrated with life.

How to Use This Workbook

The workbook will introduce you to a range of CBT skills, taught over 42 exercises.

These exercises will be divided into two main categories: cognitive techniques and behavioral techniques. You are welcome to pick and choose which exercises to complete, at your own pace and time.

Showing commitment, curiosity, and openness is important in completing these exercises. Be open to explore how you think and feel, and embrace the possibility of learning new information about yourself.

After each chapter, feel free to take a moment to reflect on what you have learned, and take down notes on the space provided.

PART 1:
CBT COGNITIVE TECHNIQUES

Chapter 2

Exploring CBT Cognitive Techniques

> The happiness of your life depends upon the quality of your thoughts.
>
> **- Marcus Aurelius**

How CBT Changes Your Thinking

There is a myth that your brain stops developing when you reach the age of 25. The human brain is actually malleable, which means that it can change based on the new information it receives. This is why you are able to pick up new habits and replace them with new ones after a few months, or develop new perspectives about the world the older you get.

The beauty about your brain being malleable is that whenever you identify negative thoughts about yourself or others, you are able to adjust them by adopting more positive and healthy thoughts. This can be done by planting new ideas into your mind and getting into the habit of challenging negative ideas and beliefs.

CBT is designed to help you restructure how you think by teaching you how to recognize faulty thoughts, known as cognitive distortions. Once you are aware of these faulty thoughts, you can adjust them to reflect reality and improve how you feel about yourself and your life.

Goals of Cognitive Techniques

Cognitive techniques are skills that are taught through CBT exercises. The main focus of these techniques is to assist with changing your thought patterns and learning how to identify negative thoughts and beliefs, before they trigger strong emotions like anxiety or depression. These skills will also empower you to take charge of your thoughts, instead of allowing your thoughts to take charge over you. You will be able to filter through true or false beliefs, and improve your perception about your life!

There are two main goals of cognitive techniques:

- To teach you how to identify specific problems in your everyday life.
- To teach you how to identify negative thoughts and reframe them in a way that supports your mental well-being.

The following chapter will explore the first goal: discovering how to identify problems in your daily life.

Chapter 3

The problem is not the problem. The problem is your attitude about the problem.

-Captain Jack Sparrow

12 Exercises to Identify Specific Problems in Your Daily Life

5 Exercises to Improve Your Memory About the Past

The brain processes about 70,000 thoughts per day. Yes, that's 70,000!

Some of these thoughts, the ones considered important to remember, are stored in long-term memory, and the rest are either discarded (like seeing a random poster on the street), or stored in short-term memory.

If I ask you about your past childhood, there are certain bits of information you will remember off the bat, and others that won't even cross your mind. Perhaps that information was discarded by your brain, or stored deep in the vaults of your long-term memory.

What also makes it difficult to remember certain things is the fact that we tend to remember what we choose to. For example, you might recall falling off the swing when you were three years old because it was such a painful experience, but forget that the same event happened four years later because you weren't as bruised the second time around.

The brain also does a sneaky trick where it causes us to remember mostly negative experiences, and either forget or downplay the positive experiences. This is called negative bias, a neurological process that you aren't even aware is happening. This is why improving your memory about the past is so important-you get to reflect on the good, bad, and ugly, and even draw valuable life lessons from the tough situations you were able to overcome!

The following exercises will take you on a trip down memory lane and help you recall various life experiences from the past.

Before and After

Think about a significant moment in your life that led to certain lifestyle changes. It could have been moving to a different school, starting puberty, or experiencing your parents' separation. Answer the following questions, describing life before and after the significant event.

1. *What words would you use to describe yourself before and after the event?*

Before event	After event

2. What activities or interests did you like/dislike before and after the event?

Before event	After event

3. What places would you visit before and after the event?

Before event	After event

4. Who would you mostly hang around with before and after the event?

Before event	After event

5. What were your goals before and after the event?

Before event	After event

Before event	After event

Revisiting Your Connections

Think about five people in your life. For each one, write down how you met. Try to remember the details of the occasion, and any significant milestones in your relationship. If you are no longer close, try to remember what made you grow apart.

Person 1:

_____

_____

_____

_____

_____

_____

_____

Person 2:

_____

_____

_____

_____

_____

_____

_____

Person 3:

_____

_____

_____

_____

_____

_____

_____

Person 4:

_____

_____

_____

_____

_____

_____

Person 5:

_____

_____

_____

_____

_____

_____

_____

_____

Tracing Back Your Feelings

Pick a recurring emotion in your life. This could be a pleasant emotion like hopefulness, or an unpleasant emotion like sadness. Describe the first time you ever felt this emotion and answer the following questions.

1. *Where were you?*

_____

_____

_____

_____

_____

_____

_____

_____

2. What did you do in that situation?

_____

_____

_____

_____

_____

_____

_____

_____

3. What caused the emotion in the first place?

_____

_____

_____

4. *How did you act as a result of feeling that way?*

5. *How does this emotion show up in your life today? Describe a recent situation where you felt that exact emotion.*

_____

_____

_____

_____

_____

_____

_____

_____

6. *How does this emotion affect your relationships today? Describe a recent situation where the emotion played a role in how you communicated with someone.*

_____

_____

_____

_____

_____

_____

_____

_____

Remembering Childhood Locations

Physically or mentally visit five places from your childhood. These could include your childhood home, school, local park, or best friend's house. For each place you visit, make a short diary-like entry about your experience. Focus on your perceptual experiences, like describing what you see, smell, hear, or feel.

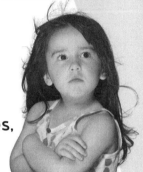

Location 1:

_____

_____

_____

_____

_____

_____

_____

Location 2:

_____

_____

_____

_____

_____

_____

_____

_____

Location 3:

_____

_____

Location 4:

_____
_____

Location 5:

_____
_____
_____
_____
_____
_____
_____

Memory Tracker

Create a memory tracker. Each time you have a random memory pop up in your head, write it down, and include details such as the date, story/situation, and how it made you feel/think. Below is a table that you can use to track your memory. The first row has been completed for you.

Date	Story/Situation	What did you think?	How did you feel?
Eg. 05/09	When I was five years old, I refused to wear any other shoes, except for my rain boots.	This memory made me think of how cheeky I was as a child.	This memory made me laugh. I feel positive.

▎▶ 3 Exercises to Understand Painful Past Events

It is normal to feel confused when thinking about past painful events in your life. Perhaps at the time when the event was taking place, you were too young to understand what was going on around you, or inside of you. As you have grown up, the memory may still be foggy in your brain or difficult to understand.

What often makes memories hard to pull up is the lack of information about what happened, how it affected you, and even how it may continue to influence how you see the world or interact with others. The more blanks you fill in, the easier it becomes to think about and speak about painful events from the past.

The following exercises will seek to help you piece together information about painful past events and reflect on how those events may affect you today.

Understanding Your Pain

Trauma is a psychological pain that is caused by being a part of, or witnessing something that is so overwhelming or unbelievable, to the extent that it causes you to feel stressed, anxious, hopeless, or unsafe. When you are traumatized, you may find it difficult to concentrate on daily tasks, like school work or household chores, and you may lose interest in social activities you used to love.

Do you suspect that you may be living with trauma? If so, then it is worth seeking professional support from a trauma counselor. Below are a few questions that can help you get more insight into your pain.

1. *Have you ever been exposed to any of the following experiences:*

- physical assault
- physical illness
- car accident
- losing a loved one
- child abuse
- physical abuse
- sexual abuse
- relocating to a different country
- being separated from your parents

If the answer is yes, share as much as you are comfortable with, in the space provided below.

_____

_____

_____

_____

_____

_____

_____

_____

_____

_____

2. Were you directly exposed to the trauma? E.g. Did you get physically injured?

_____

_____

_____

_____

3. Did you watch the trauma happening in your environment? E.g. Did you witness two people fighting?

_____

_____

_____

_____

4. Were you affected by the trauma indirectly? E.g. Did you hear about violence happening around your community?

_____

_____

_____

_____

5. *Were you exposed to trauma repeatedly? E.g. Did you experience more than one traumatic event, on several occasions?*

_____

_____

_____

Trauma Quiz

Another useful way to identify trauma is to learn the common physical and emotional symptoms. Trauma symptoms appear in your mind and body. They affect how you think, feel, and behave.

Complete the following chart to the best of your abilities, reflecting on the trauma-related symptoms you regularly experience, as well as how often and how long you experience them. Feel free to take this chart with you when you visit a mental healthcare provider.

Symptom	Yes/No	How often? 0 = never 1 = rarely 2 = often 3 = very often 4 = all the time	How long? 1 = several seconds 2 = several minutes 3 = a few hours 4 = a day 5 = several days 6 = more than a week
Do you have trouble remembering certain details about the event?			

Have you lost interest in the activities you used to enjoy before the event?			
Do you avoid activities that remind you of the event?			
Do you think about yourself or others negatively?			
Do you perform more risky behaviors, like smoking, drinking, or having sex, now than you did before the event?			
Do you have a hard time thinking positively?			
Do you blame yourself for the event?			
Do you have nightmares about the event?			
Do you feel isolated from other people?			
Do you avoid thinking about the future?			

Creating Your Safe Place

A safe place can be a physical or mental location that you visit whenever you are feeling overwhelmed. You can think of it as your private sanctuary, where you feel emotionally safe. When you are living in stressful conditions or going through stressful situations, you can retreat to your safe place and enjoy some uninterrupted time to yourself.

Below are a few questions that will help you identify your physical safe place.

1. *List the places where you feel the safest. E.g. Your bedroom, garden shed, library, etc. Mention the qualities of those places that make them feel so secure.*

_____

_____

_____

_____

_____

_____

2. List a number of activities that you enjoy, which make you feel calm. Be sure to bring a box of these activities (or materials) to your safe place.

_____

_____

_____

_____

_____

3. List a few people who make you feel safe. Describe how these people play a role in your life. Note, when you are feeling overwhelmed, you are welcome to reach out to your safe people.

_____

_____

_____

_____

_____

4. What sensations do you desire to feel in your safe place? E.g. Do you want to feel relaxed, accepted, or free?

_____

_____

_____

_____

_____

_____

5. Create an action plan for designing your safe place. E.g. What art supplies, furniture, posters, music, or other resources will you need to turn an ordinary space into a safe space? Make sure that you get the permission from your parents, teachers, or local authorities before you get situated.

_____

_____

_____

_____

_____

4 Exercises to Treat Depersonalization

One of the less spoken about symptoms of anxiety or stress is an experience known as depersonalization. It can be described as an out-of-body experience that causes you to question reality, or feel like you are an actor or actress playing the role as you. Life starts to feel like one long dream that you can't seem to wake up from.

When you are experiencing depersonalization, you may find it difficult to process emotions, but maintain heightened alertness. You may feel numb or detached to what is happening in your life, and struggle to respond to everyday situations with an appropriate reaction.

For example, you may not show any warm and fuzzy emotions toward your family, pay attention at school, or act silly and joke around with your friends like you used to do. In a sense, you act like a detached observer who is watching your life playing around in front of them, but not participating.

If you can relate to any of these symptoms, the following exercises will help you regain some feeling and begin the journey of reconnecting to yourself, and your life. To get a full examination of your symptoms, please consult a qualified mental health doctor.

Depersonalization Quiz

Are you wondering if you have ever experienced depersonalization before? This short quiz will take you through some statements representing the symptoms of depersonalization. Answer yes or no, as well as how often and for how long you experience the symptoms. Once again, feel free to take the completed quiz with you when you consult with a doctor.

Symptom	Yes/No	How often? 0 = never 1 = rarely 2 = often 3 = very often 4 = all the time	How long? 1 = several seconds 2 = several minutes 3 = a few hours 4 = a day 5 = several days 6 = more than a week
I feel a big, empty hole inside of me.			
I feel like I have lost the essence of my personality.			

I feel like I am standing on the sidelines of my life, observing everything taking place.			
My actions and behaviors are stiff and regimented. I remember acting spontaneously.			
I pay a lot of attention to my thoughts and body sensations.			
I don't cry, laugh, or feel pain.			
I don't feel anything in stressful situations.			
I don't have hobbies or passions. Nothing really interests me.			
I don't feel affection toward my friends and family.			
I feel like I may have an illness that is not being treated.			

Flipping Through Your Gallery

Bring out a photo of you from many years ago. Look at the photo and remind yourself of what was happening in your life during the time. Enjoy the experience of reconnecting to a younger version of yourself. You can use the following questions to jog your memory.

1. *Where were you when this photo was being taken? Does the location have any significance to you? For example, was it the family home where you spent a large portion of your childhood?*

_____

_____

_____

_____

_____

2. Who else is in the photo with you? If nobody is visible, who was taking the photo? What kind of relationship did you have with that person at the time? For example, was the person your best friend, or a stranger passing on the road?

_____

_____

_____

_____

_____

3. What is happening in the photo? For example, were you celebrating a birthday? Or on vacation with your family?

_____

_____

_____

_____

4. *What do you remember about that specific day? Was it a good or bad day? Do you remember being happy? Was there any conflict that took place?*

_____

_____

_____

_____

_____

5. *Looking at the younger version of yourself, what do you think you wanted to say at that specific time in your life that you never got the chance to? For example, would you have appreciated support? Did you desire to see your family getting along?*

_____

_____

_____

_____

_____

_____

Choose another photo and answer the same questions. This time, go back deeper into your past, and see what else you can remember about the younger version of yourself.

Reconnect With Your Body

A great way to treat depersonalization is to feel your own body move! Physical activity gently helps you focus on what is happening in the present moment. The flexing of your muscles or movement of your legs lets you know that your experience is real, and you are in control of your body. The best part is that you don't need to engage in intense physical activity to see positive results. All you need is 15 minutes of moderate cardio exercise (i.e. Playing a sport, doing an aerobic workout, dancing, or taking a walk), three times a week.

When you have completed each workout session, record your experience in the table below. The first row has been completed for you.

Date	Type of physical activity	Post-workout, my body feels...	Post-workout, I think and feel...
E.g. 05/09	Tennis	My arms and thighs feel heavy, but not sore.	I had so much fun. I feel excited for my next tennis session.

Date	Type of physical activity	Post-workout, my body feels...	Post-workout, I think and feel...

Verify Reality With Your Senses

When you begin to doubt your reality, it is important to ground yourself with facts about your experience. In other words, your goal is to find enough evidence to prove that you are real and that what you are experiencing is real.

To do this, you will need to activate your five senses (i.e. sight, smell, taste, touch, and hearing). You can decide whether to complete this exercise indoors or outdoors. Always go for the environment that feels safe and comfortable for you. Next, begin to notice what you can see, feel, hear, taste, and smell. Write down your observations on the table provided below.

For example, if you have decided to visit your local park, you could make the following observations:

- **Sight:** Kids are playing on the swings.
- **Hearing:** Birds are chirping.
- **Touch:** A cool breeze is moving swiftly past my face.
- **Smell:** I smell wet grass.
- **Taste:** I can taste what I still had for breakfast.

The first row has been completed for you.

Locations	Sight	Hearing	Touch	Smell	Taste
E.g. Shopping mall	People walking past me.	Sound of trolleys.	My clothing fabric.	Cologne	Coffee.

Locations	Sight	Hearing	Touch	Smell	Taste

Now that you are able to identify specific problems in your life, it is time to move on to the second goal: becoming aware of unproductive thought patterns.

Chapter 4

11 Exercises to Become Aware of Unproductive Thought Patterns

> For there is nothing either good or bad, but thinking makes it so.
>
> **-Shakespeare**

4 Exercises to Recognize and Empathize With Intrusive Thoughts

Intrusive thoughts are negative thoughts that enter your mind without any prior warning, and cause a lot of stress and anxiety. For example, you could be sitting in class doing your work, and all of a sudden, a strange or scary thought appears in your mind. From that point onward, you may find it difficult to concentrate on your class work, or engage with your peers as normal.

The amount of distress that intrusive thoughts cause depends on how you react to them. For instance, someone who takes an intrusive thought seriously, and believes that whatever they have imagined is true, or will happen, then they might react with strong emotions, like fear or anger.

The types of intrusive thoughts that can appear in your mind range in degree of intensity. Common types of intrusive thoughts include:

☺ Inappropriate thoughts about sex.

☺ Imagining yourself or a loved one being killed.

☺ Having suicidal thoughts.

☺ Fear of contracting a terminal illness.

☺ Thoughts about committing a violent act toward yourself or others.

☺ Fear that people are mocking or gossiping about you behind your back.

☺ Worrying that you are a burden on others.

You may feel ashamed for having these unwanted or socially unacceptable thoughts, but it is important to know that they are common and many people experience them from time to time. So, don't be alarmed. You are not going crazy!

When seeking to manage intrusive thoughts, your job is to recognize when they tend to arise, what triggers them, and find healthy coping strategies. The following exercises will teach you how to identify and empathize with your intrusive thoughts.

Thought Diary

It is comforting to write down the kinds of intrusive thoughts you experience on a regular basis. This can help you anticipate them, so that when they do eventually arise, you are not left feeling confused or shocked.

Record every intrusive thought you have on the table below, describing the main theme, your initial response, and how you handled yourself (with a rating out of five). The first row has been done for you.

Intrusive thought	Main theme	Initial response	How I handled myself (1 = unsuccessful, 5 = very successful)
E.g. I don't deserve to eat.	Self-harm	I felt guilty, but managed to continue eating my lunch.	I was proud of the fact that I didn't let the thought talk me out of eating. Rating: 4

Intrusive thought	Main theme	Initial response	How I handled myself (1 = unsuccessful, 5 = very successful)

Empathizing With Your Intrusive Thoughts

Think about a significant moment in your life that led to certain lifestyle changes. It could have been moving to a different school, starting puberty, or experiencing your parents' separation. Answer the following questions, describing life before and after the significant event.

Copy the intrusive thoughts that you wrote down for the previous exercise, and next to each one, write down the unprocessed emotions those thoughts may be revealing.

Intrusive thought	Unprocessed emotion
E.g. Worry that people are always gossiping about me.	This thought may be revealing my deeper insecurities about not being likable as a person, and the constant need to gain others' approval.

Intrusive thought	Unprocessed emotion

Challenging Intrusive Thoughts

When an intrusive thought appears in your mind, remind yourself that you don't have to accept it as the truth, or being your reality. The questions below will help you challenge the validity of your intrusive thoughts and put your mind at ease.

Think about a recurring intrusive thought that has been bothering you and answer the following questions:

1. *What evidence do you have that your thought is true?*

_____

_____

_____

_____

_____

_____

2. What evidence do you have that your thought is false?

_____

_____

_____

_____

_____

3. Would you describe your thought as rigid, flexible, or balanced?

_____

_____

_____

_____

_____

4. *Does your thought match reality, or does it distort reality?*

_____

_____

_____

_____

_____

5. *Does your thought encourage healthy feelings and behaviors?*

_____

_____

_____

_____

_____

6. *Would you encourage a friend to think this way?*

_____

_____

_____

_____

_____

Inner Critic vs. Inner Advocate

There is a part of you that is extremely judgmental about everything you do, but there is also another part of you that is extremely compassionate about everything you do. These inner voices are known as the inner critic and inner advocate.

Whenever an intrusive thought appears, get into the habit of questioning the voice of the inner critic and supporting the voice of the inner advocate. For example, you might find evidence proving the inner critic to be false, while finding positive beliefs to support the inner advocate.

Complete the following table to practice disempowering the inner critic and empowering the inner advocate. The first row has been done for you.

Intrusive thought	Evidence to prove my thought is false	Unprocessed emotions behind my thought	Positive take away from my thought	Positive belief to replace my thought
E.g. I'm ugly and no one will ever date me.	I have beautiful round eyes, clear skin, and a charming smile.	Feeling of unworthiness	I need to spend more time reminding myself how beautiful I am.	My beauty is rare, which makes it that much more valuable.

Intrusive thought	Evidence to prove my thought is false	Unprocessed emotions behind my thought	Positive take away from my thought	Positive belief to replace my thought

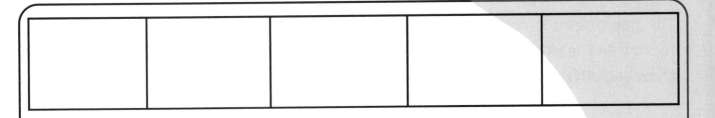

7 Exercises to Challenge Negative Thinking Patterns

Negative thinking is simply contaminated thinking. The rational thought process, which follows the ABC format, is distorted to reflect conclusions that are not based on facts or reality. The ABC format goes like this:

Activating event: You go through a personal experience, which leads to...

Belief/thought: Searching for a rule, belief, attitude, expectation, or meaning that can help you interpret what you have experienced. This will ultimately cause you to...

Consequences (emotional and behavioral): Respond with an appropriate action, feeling, or body sensation.

Imagine that this format was contaminated with information that doesn't follow sound logic, such as an assumption that isn't based on facts. You would still have the personal experience, but how you interpret it, and the emotional response or action that you take would not match reality.

For example, you might respond with rage when you assume that someone is criticizing you, when the appropriate action was to verify the facts and seek clarity. Or you might shut people out of your life because you believe that people can't be trusted, when the appropriate response would be to see human beings as individuals and get to learn about new acquaintances before judging their character.

The good news is negative thinking can be corrected by understanding the ABC format and learning how to challenge your thoughts. The following exercises will show you different ways for you to do that!

Connecting the Dots With ABC

Below are examples of a few "activating events" that trigger thought patterns. Go through each row and write down your typical belief/thought and consequence that often follows each activating event.

The purpose of this exercise is to help you understand how an ordinary life event can influence how you feel and behave. The first row has been completed for you.

Activating event	Belief/thought	Consequences
E.g. Getting disciplined by your parents.	My parents want to make my life miserable.	Deliberately going against their rules as an act of protest.
Failing a test at school.		
Seeing a group of people staring at you.		
Speaking to your crush for the first time.		

Activating event	Belief/thought	Consequences
Being told that your athletic skills need work.		
Not receiving any "likes" on your social media post.		
Noticing that your parents are in a bad mood.		
Being blue ticked by one of your friends.		
Not getting along with certain groups of people.		
Experiencing family conflict at home.		

Finding Balance

Negative thoughts can sometimes adopt an all-or-nothing type of thinking. For example, you might see someone as being good or evil, but overlook the fact that people have good and bad days, strengths and weaknesses. One of the ways of correcting negative thoughts is to find a more balanced way of thinking about the situation, which is neither extremely positive nor extremely negative.

Go through the negative thoughts presented in the table below and think about a fair or balanced perspective to replace the thought with. The first row has been completed for you.

Negative thought	Fair/balanced thought
E.g. There's no point in going to college because I will probably fail.	Sure, college will require a lot more out of me than high school. However, by the time I get there, I will have the necessary skills and knowledge to handle new academic challenges.

Negative thought	Fair/balanced thought

Negative thought	Fair/balanced thought

Setting Goals to Combat Negative Thinking

In order to eliminate negative thought patterns, you need to set goals to motivate and remind you of the quality of thoughts you desire! Setting goals can also help you be proactive in practicing CBT cognitive exercises and tracking your progress.

Below are some questions to help you set positive thinking goals.

1. *What is the negative thought you are seeking to change?*

_____

_____

_____

_____

_____

2. How is this thought causing problems in your life?

_____

_____

_____

_____

_____

3. What healthy thoughts would you like to think instead? Note: These will be the goals you work toward.

_____

_____

_____

_____

_____

4. *How will you need to change your thinking in order to achieve your goal?*

_____

_____

_____

_____

_____

5. *List a number of goal-related tasks (not more than five) that you can practice regularly to achieve your goal. Make sure that the tasks are realistic, and manageable.*

_____

_____

_____

_____

_____

6. *What are the potential benefits of achieving your goal?*

_____

_____

_____

_____

_____

7. *What necessary skills or resources do you need to achieve your goal?*

_____

_____

_____

_____

_____

8. *Who can you lean on for support?*

_____

_____

_____

_____

_____

9. *When can you get started working toward your goal?*

_____

_____

_____

_____

_____

10. What days and times of the week can you commit to carrying goal-related tasks?

_____

_____

_____

_____

11. How will you know when you have achieved your goal? What signs or results can you look out for?

_____

_____

_____

_____

Shifting From Problem-Seer to Problem-Solver

While it is good to learn how to identify negative thinking patterns, it shouldn't be the only thing you do. After a negative thought is identified, your next step should be finding a reasonable solution (one that is within your control). This will ensure that you don't feel "stuck" whenever you catch yourself thinking negatively.

Below is a table with negative thoughts that present potential problems. Look at each problem and think about simple solutions that can improve the real or imagined situation.

Negative thought + Problem	Potential solution
E.g. My parents are mad at me.	I can approach my parents and ask if everything is okay.
I'm not going to pass the upcoming exam.	
I don't think my new group of friends like me.	

Negative thought + Problem	Potential solution
I'm too fat to wear this outfit.	
My crush is ignoring me, which means that they are just not interested.	
I feel depressed when I get on social media.	
My social life is non-existent.	
I have nobody to talk to about my personal problems.	
I'm the least attractive person in my friend group.	
I don't have the confidence to make new friends.	

Rate Your Problems

Sometimes, negative thinking is triggered by feeling overwhelmed with life. Let's face it-life doesn't always go smoothly, and at times, you are faced with tough challenges that cause you to feel afraid, doubtful, or discouraged.

When life starts to feel "too much," you can write down the issues you are facing and rate their degree of intensity. This can help you manage how much headspace you give to each problem.

Below is a table that you can use to write down various problems you are faced with. Next to each problem, give it a score out of 5, indicate whether it is within your control to change (or not), and the solution you can carry out. The first row has been completed for you.

Problem	How intense does it feel? (1 = tolerable, 5 = unbearable)	Is it within or outside your control?	Potential solutions to bring relief
E.g. I am very shy, and this affects my ability to make friends.	3.5	Within my control	Join an age-appropriate forum and practice striking conversations with others. Join an interest-based social group.
			Spend more time catching up with old friends or cousins my age to build confidence.

Problem	How intense does it feel? (1 = tolerable, 5 = unbearable)	Is it within or outside your control?	Potential solutions to bring relief

Problem	How intense does it feel? (1 = tolerable, 5 = unbearable)	Is it within or outside your control?	Potential solutions to bring relief

Identify Emotion-Based Thinking

Emotional reasoning is a thinking error that occurs when you confuse how you feel about something as being the facts about the situation. For example, if you feel ignored by your friend, you might think they are upset with you. On the contrary, the real reason could be something different, like your friend being preoccupied with school work. Emotional reasoning can be dangerous because it leads you to make untrue conclusions about a situation.

The following questions will help you challenge emotion-based judgments.

1. *Think about a recent event or belief about something/someone, which has upset you, and write it down below. E.g Arguing with your best friend.*

---

2. What strong emotion does this event or belief bring up? E.g. Feeling judged.

_____

_____

_____

_____

_____

3. How might your strong emotion lead you to distort the facts? E.g. Since I feel judged, I might think that my friend was deliberately trying to hurt me.

_____

_____

_____

4. *What facts could you be ignoring because of your strong emotion? E.g. I could be ignoring the fact that my friend is trying to give me advice because they have experienced something similar in their life.*

_____

_____

_____

_____

_____

5. *If you give yourself enough time to process your emotion, how differently might you view the situation? E.g. I might be able to see that my friend is coming from a place of love, and they want the best for me.*

_____

_____

Avoid Creating Expectations

It is normal to feel angry or suspicious when somebody fails to live up to your expectations. For example, if you expected your crush to text you in the morning and they failed to do so, you might think they are showing inconsistency, a lack of interest, or undermining your sense of self-worth.

All of these negative thoughts come from expecting others to hold the same beliefs, attitudes, and behaviors as you. This type of thinking is unfair because everybody has their own way of thinking, feeling, and making decisions. None of us can control how another person acts—we can only control our own actions.

Therefore, while it is good to have standards, they should be treated as preferences, rather than demands when concerning other people. Doing this will allow you to be more flexible in how you deal with unmet needs and desires. For example, even if your crush doesn't text you in the morning, you are able to adjust to their routine without feeling rejected.

Answer the following questions to challenge the expectations you have of others.

1. Think of someone who you are on bad terms with because of an expectation they failed to meet. Describe what the expectations were.

_____

_____

_____

_____

_____

2. When creating the expectations, were you mindful of the fact that the other person might have different rules, values, or mindset about life? Provide evidence.

_____

_____

_____

_____

_____

3. *Would it be possible to keep your standards, while allowing the other person to have their own standards too? If so, describe how that might look like in your relationship?*

_____

_____

_____

_____

_____

4. *Which demands are you willing to turn into preferences?*

_____

_____

_____

_____

_____

5. *What are you not willing to compromise on? Note: It is okay to set boundaries with others.*

_____

_____

_____

_____

_____

_____

You have completed the first part of the workbook, congratulations! So far, we have explored CBT cognitive techniques, by focusing on two goals: identifying specific problems and negative thought patterns. The second part of the workbook will teach you useful CBT behavioral techniques that can assist you in changing unwanted behaviors.

PART 2:
CBT BEHAVIORAL TECHNIQUES

Chapter 5

When you replace "Why is this happening to me?" with "What is this trying to teach me?" everything shifts.

- Anne Dennish

Exploring CBT Behavioral Techniques

▶ How CBT Changes Your Behavior

In the first part of the workbook, you learned how to recognize and change negative thoughts into more balanced and rational thoughts. But since negative thoughts are connected to negative feelings and actions, changing your thinking must lead to positive behaviors changes too!

For example, you may have previously believed that people can't be trusted, but with some CBT work, adjusted your thought to reflect a more balanced view, such as "Each person has strengths and weaknesses." After making the adjustment, your --

attitude and behaviors toward others would effectively change.

Instead of being suspicious of new acquaintances, and as a result being guarded, you would be more open to get to know them and find out what they are like, and whether you have something in common.

CBT is therefore a useful tool to encourage changes in both your thinking and behaviors, and teach you how to recognize negative habits and replace them with positive ones!

Goals of Behavioral Techniques

Behavioral techniques are skills that are reinforced through CBT exercises. The main focus is to help you understand the impact of your behaviors, and find better ways to regulate your emotions, improve your self-control, and find healthier ways to cope with stress.

There are two main goals of behavioral techniques:

- To teach you how to name, describe, and cope with strong emotions.
- To teach you how to identify impulsive behaviors.

The following chapter will explore the first goal: discovering how to name, describe, and cope with strong emotions.

Chapter 6

I don't want to be at the mercy of my emotions. I want to use them, to enjoy them, and to dominate them.

-Oscar Wilde

11 Naming, Describing, and Coping Strategies for Embracing Strong Emotions

4 Activities to Identify and Name Emotions

What often makes strong emotions difficult to manage is the lack of awareness about what you are actually feeling. For instance, you might notice that your mood has changed, but unable to tell what exactly you are feeling. Some of the easier emotions to describe are sadness, anger, or happiness, but even these emotions can sometimes be too vague when expressing how you truly feel.

Learning how to identify and name your emotions can reduce the anxiety that tends to arise when you sense a strong feeling, but don't know what it is. Instead of being afraid of your emotions, you can explore what they are and what they might be trying to communicate about your experience.

Furthermore, once you acknowledge your emotions, it is easier to tame them and think of healthy coping strategies to reduce the intensity and return to your normal state. The following exercises will teach you how to identify and name your emotions.

Expand Your Emotions Vocabulary

The first step to understanding your emotions is to learn the right terminology. There are hundreds of different types of emotions you can feel, which are grouped under six primary emotions: happiness, anger, sadness, fear, surprise, and disgust.

For example, while it is acceptable to feel sad, you may find that your sadness leans more toward feeling lonely, rather than feeling discouraged. Both loneliness and discouragement fall under the sadness category; however, they describe two different kinds of experiences. This is the beauty of expanding your emotions vocabulary-you get to describe your feelings as close as possible to how they are experienced in your body.

Look at the table of emotions below and answer the questions that follow.

Happy	Angry	Sad	Fearful	Surprised	Disgusted
Cheerful	Bitter	Lonely	Anxious	Energized	Guilty
Peaceful	Frustrated	Disappointed	Cautious	Excited	Embarrassed

Happy	Angry	Sad	Fearful	Surprised	Disgusted
Grateful	Annoyed	Depressed	Insecure	Curious	Inferior
Hopeful	Impatient	Heartbroken	Nervous	Shocked	Ignored
Loved	Insulted	Discouraged	Tearful	Playful	Unaccepted
Optimistic	Jealous	Neglected	Uncomfortable	Passionate	Ugly
Satisfied	Spiteful	Hopeless	Lost/confused	Enchanted	Ashamed

Based on the table above:

1. *Describe how you felt on your first day at kindergarten.*

_____

_____

_____

_____

_____

2. If you could describe the relationship you have with your best friend, what words would you use?

_____

_____

_____

_____

_____

3. Think about a challenging life event you have overcome, like changing schools or getting injured. Describe how you felt at the time and how you were able to pick yourself up.

_____

_____

_____

_____

_____

4. *If you could describe how you feel about the future, what words would you use, and why?*

_____

_____

_____

_____

_____

5. *Describe your relationship with a difficult person in your life. It could be a difficult school teacher or family member. What words would you use to describe how you feel about the relationship? Furthermore, what words would you use to describe how you desire to feel?*

_____

_____

_____

_____

Exploring Your Primary Emotions

The great thing about emotions is that they are temporary and ever-changing. For instance, the sadness you feel today could morph into happiness tomorrow, and maybe fear the following week.

When your emotions change, it is not a sign of going crazy. It is simply your body's way of keeping you updated on the emotional impact of various situations occurring in your life.

You can take emotions as feedback and track patterns in how you are feeling. This will give you a good indication of the state of your mental health, and whether you may need to reach out for some support. The following exercise will help you get more familiar with the six primary emotions and notice how they have shown up in your life.

Happiness

Happiness is the state of being satisfied and thankful for your life. Answer the questions below to explore your relationship with happiness.

1. *Describe a moment of pure happiness that you remember.*

_____

_____

_____

_____

_____

2. *What did you do in that situation? How do you remember acting?*

_____

_____

_____

_____

3. How do you notice when other people are happy? What are the signs?

_____

_____

_____

_____

_____

4. How does being happy affect your relationship with others?

_____

_____

_____

_____

_____

Anger

Anger is the state of feeling annoyed or bitter about something or the actions of someone. Answer the questions below to explore your relationship with anger.

1. *Describe a moment of intense anger that you remember.*

_____

_____

_____

_____

_____

2. *What did you do in that situation? How do you remember acting?*

_____

_____

_____

_____

3. *How do you notice when other people are angry? What are the signs?*

_____

_____

_____

_____

4. *How does being angry affect your relationship with others?*

_____

_____

_____

_____

Fear

Fear arises when you feel threatened by real or imagined danger. Answer the questions below to explore your relationship with fear.

1. *Describe a moment of fear that you remember.*

_____

_____

_____

_____

_____

2. *What did you do in that situation? How do you remember acting?*

_____

_____

_____

_____

_____

_____

3. *How do you notice when other people are fearful? What are the signs?*

_____

_____

_____

_____

_____

_____

4. *How does being fearful affect your relationship with others?*

_____

_____

_____

_____

_____

_____

▶ Sadness

Sadness is a state of being at a loss or mourning something terrible that has happened. Answer the questions below to explore your relationship with sadness.

1. *Describe a moment of immense sadness that you remember.*

_____

_____

_____

_____

2. *What did you do in that situation? How do you remember acting?*

_____

_____

_____

_____

_____

3. *How do you notice when other people are sad? What are the signs?*

_____

_____

_____

_____

_____

_____

4. *How does being sad affect your relationship with others?*

_____

_____

_____

_____

_____

Surprise

Surprise is the state of being stunned about something unexpected happening in your life. Answer the questions below to explore your relationship with surprise.

1. *Describe a moment of surprise that you remember.*

_____

_____

_____

_____

_____

2. *What did you do in that situation? How do you remember acting?*

_____

_____

_____

_____

_____

3. *How do you notice when other people are surprised? What are the signs?*

_____

_____

_____

_____

_____

4. *How does being surprised affect your relationship with others?*

_____

_____

_____

_____

_____

Disgust

Disgust is the feeling of strong disapproval of something or someone, or feeling like others strongly disapprove of you. Answer the questions below to explore your relationship with disgust.

1. *Describe a moment of disgust that you remember.*

_____

_____

_____

_____

2. *What did you do in that situation? How do you remember acting?*

_____

_____

_____

_____

_____

3. *How do you notice when other people are disgusted? What are the signs?*

_____

_____

_____

_____

_____

4. *How does being disgusted affect your relationship with others?*

_____

_____

_____

_____

_____

Understanding Your Emotions When You Are Upset

Managing your emotions is incredibly difficult when you are upset. To have more control of your behaviors, especially when upset, it is crucial to speak about how you are feeling, or at least write your feelings down on paper. This will prevent you from making impulsive decisions that cause more pain to yourself or others.

Below are a few questions that can help you understand the impact of your emotions when you are upset.

1. *Describe a recent situation that made you upset. What happened? How did the situation start, unfold, and end?*

_____

_____

_____

_____

_____

_____

2. How did the situation make you feel? Describe the emotions that you felt.

_____

_____

_____

_____

_____

3. What external events led up to the situation? In other words, mention the actions of others that contributed to the situation.

_____

_____

_____

_____

_____

4. *What negative thoughts might have made the situation feel more intense than it actually was? In other words, mention the type of unhelpful thoughts that were distorting how you viewed the situation or people involved.*

_____

_____

_____

_____

_____

5. *How did you behave as a result of how you felt at the time? What decisions/actions did you make?*

_____

_____

_____

_____

6. What were the consequences of your decisions/actions later?

_____

_____

_____

_____

_____

7. What healthy coping strategies could you have adopted that might have helped you in the situation? Place a tick next to the coping strategy you believe may have been useful.

Coping strategy	Tick (X)
Communicate what I am feeling.	
Excuse myself from the conversation and walk away.	

Coping strategy	Tick (X)
Notice my feelings and take deep breaths.	
Set an immediate boundary.	
Adjust my expectations and be willing to compromise.	
Find some humor in the situation.	
Be more assertive and speak up for my needs and rights.	
Engage in positive self-talk and show myself compassion.	
Validate the other person's experience and make them feel heard.	
Look for support before or after the situation.	

Rating Your Emotional Experience

The incorrect assumption is to think that every strong emotion is felt with the greatest intensity. This is not true. Strong emotions often range in intensity, depending on the situation you are in.

For example, on a scale of 1-10 (1 being very dull and 10 being very strong), different situations can make you feel a different intensity of anger. You might rate missing a school deadline as a 4/10, and being betrayed by a close friend as an 8/10.

Being able to rate the intensity of your strong emotions can help you tame them in the heat of the moment.

The following exercise will focus on rating situations that make you angry out of a scale of 1-10.

Situation	Anger rating from 1-10 (1 = very dull, 10 = very strong)
Being interrupted while you are speaking.	
Having your text message blue-ticked (left on read).	

Situation	Anger rating from 1-10 (1 = very dull, 10 = very strong)
Experiencing verbal attacks (i.e. insults, name calling) during an argument.	
Having your boundaries violated.	
Hearing "no" from someone.	
Having plans canceled last minute.	
Failing a test you studied hard for.	
Being self-critical about your performance at school.	
Feeling like your needs are not being considered.	
Not receiving support from others.	

7 Exercises to Regulate Your Strong Emotions

Emotional regulation is one of the core CBT skills that can improve your ability to control your feelings and actions during stressful situations. In general, regulating strong emotions is not easy because doing so requires you to deny your natural instinct, which is to emotionally attack, withdraw, or shut down. However, with greater self-awareness and self-regulation techniques like being mindful of how you are feeling, you can become better at observing your strong emotions and managing them in healthier ways.

The following exercises will teach you several positive strategies to regulate your emotions, which include reappraising the situation, becoming more assertive and less aggressive, and identifying alternative behaviors.

Distract Yourself From Your Feelings

There are certain times when entertaining specific emotions can be seen as inappropriate. For example, before a big exam, focusing on your anxious feelings can throw you off. Please note that this doesn't mean that you should disregard some feelings, but instead postpone them to a more appropriate time. After your exam, for example, you can spend 15 minutes journaling about how you felt before and during the test, and what you did to calm yourself down.

Finding the right distraction can be a great coping strategy when you don't have the time to process your strong emotions.

Look at the table below and provide examples of positive distractions when overcome with strong emotions. The first row has been completed for you.

Scenario	Positive distraction
E.g. You feel nervous before standing up to say a speech/give a presentation.	Think of the valuable information you are going to share with the class and how excited they are to learn from you.

Scenario	Positive distraction
You notice yourself becoming angry while listening to your parents speak about your behavior.	
You feel insecure while hanging out with a group of people you think are better than you.	
You speak negatively about your body, which makes you fear going out with friends.	
After getting a bad test mark, you go on a rant about how stupid you are.	
An opportunity has been presented to you, but you doubt your abilities to succeed.	
You hesitate sharing your ideas with others because of being afraid of judgment.	

Meditation to Sit With Strong Emotions

Meditation is an Eastern practice that is popularly used in the West to calm the mind and body. There are different types of meditations, but what they all have in common is the ability to direct your focus on something, whether it is on a specific object, thought, or sensation. This process has a calming effect and can reduce stress and anxiety.

The following meditation is known as a mindfulness meditation. The aim is to bring your attention to whatever strong thoughts or feelings flowing in and out of your mind. After practicing this meditation, reflect on your experience and what insights you gained.

▌ Instructions:

☺ Sit in a comfortable position on a chair.

☺ Make sure that your back is supported, shoulders dropped, and arms resting comfortably on your lap.

☺ Close your eyes and take a deep breath through your nose. Hold it for a few seconds, then let it out of your mouth, slowly. Repeat this breathing pattern until you are relaxed.

☺ Focus your attention on your head and continue breathing normally. Imagine that you entered your mind and got the privilege to watch your emotions. Picture your mind as a blue sky, and your emotions as white clouds passing by.

😊 Simply observe each cloud entering from the right and slowly floating across your mind, until disappearing on the left. Notice how some emotions are much larger, and take longer to fade away than others.

😊 Feel free to stop any emotion you like, and look at it closely. Give the emotion a name, and figure out how it makes you feel. Avoid judging the emotion as being good or bad. Embrace it and try to learn as much as you can.

😊 Notice the effect that some emotions have on your body. For example, do some emotions increase your heart beat? Do they give you a burst of energy? Now notice the effect that some emotions have on your mind. Identify the kinds of thoughts they trigger in your mind, and how intense these thoughts feel.

😊 Remember to breathe through uncomfortable emotions and feel free to let go of them at any given point. Once you have given an emotion cloud enough attention, move onto the next one.

😊 To end the meditation, imagine your mind has been cleared of all emotion clouds, and you are simply enjoying the endless blue sky. Enjoy the neutral feeling of "nothing," and gently open your eyes when you are ready.

On the line space provided below, reflect on your meditation. How was the experience for you? Which emotions came to your mind, and what did you learn from them?

_____

_____

_____

_____

Letter to Your Younger Self

Think back to a time in your childhood, when you felt a strong emotion but didn't know how to process it, or who to talk to about it. Write a letter to that younger version of yourself and help them through the emotion.

Use the skills you have learned so far to teach them how to cope with that emotion. Make sure that your letter uses positive and encouraging words that bring comfort to that little kid.

_____

_____

_____

_____

_____

_____

Anticipating Strong Emotions

Did you know that you can anticipate a strong emotion and take action before it fully emerges? This is possible when you identify the emotional triggers that cause you to feel certain ways. Below is a table with different types of strong emotions.

Next to each emotion, write down the types of beliefs, memories, environmental cues that trigger you to feel that specific way. The first row has been done for you.

Strong emotion	Belief trigger (e.g. What you think)	Memory trigger (e.g. What happened in the past)	Environment trigger (e.g. What is happening now)
E.g. Shame	"I'm not a good person."	Being alienated from my group of friends. Being bullied in primary school.	Being raised by an angry parent who constantly criticizes me. Comparing my personality to other kids on TikTok.
Anxiety			

Strong emotion	Belief trigger (e.g. What you think)	Memory trigger (e.g. What happened in the past)	Environment trigger (e.g. What is happening now)
Jealousy			
Self-doubt			
Lonely			
Judgmental			
Betrayed			
Isolated			

Helpful and Harmful Emotional Reactions

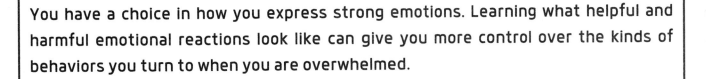

All emotions are valid and deserve to be felt, however they can be expressed in helpful and harmful ways. For instance, anger can help you build or tear down relationships, depending on how you express it. The helpful side of anger is being firm about your boundaries and enforcing consequences when others violate them. The harmful side of anger is yelling and cursing at someone who does something to offend you.

You have a choice in how you express strong emotions. Learning what helpful and harmful emotional reactions look like can give you more control over the kinds of behaviors you turn to when you are overwhelmed.

Look at the table below and write down examples of helpful and harmful ways of expressing strong emotions. The first row has been completed for you.

Strong emotion	Harmful reaction	Helpful reaction
E.g. Insecurity	Projecting my low self-esteem onto others by being nasty and judgmental.	Spending time correcting my negative self-talk and focusing on my character strengths.

Strong emotion	Harmful reaction	Helpful reaction
Loneliness		
Bitterness		
Discouragement		
Worry		
Revengeful		
Embarrassment		
Depressed		

Behavior Test

When strong emotions come quickly, you can feel confused about what just happened or how you are feeling. In those moments, you can distract your mind by performing a quick behavior test to remind yourself of what set off the strong emotion and how you are currently feeling.

When strong emotions have you feeling disoriented, retreat to a quiet space and answer the following question:

1. *Describe what happened objectively. Mention only what you saw and heard.*

_____

_____

_____

_____

_____

2. What did you do at that moment? Describe the decision you made, or actions you took.

_____

_____

_____

_____

_____

3. Did your behavior fit with a helpful emotion? In other words, did your behavior improve or worsen the situation?

_____

_____

_____

_____

_____

4. Based on your actions, what strong emotion(s) do you believe you were feeling?

_____

_____

_____

_____

_____

5. In future, how might you express this emotion in a helpful way?

_____

_____

_____

_____

_____

Control Your Urges

Sometimes, strong emotions can tempt you to respond in harmful ways, like rebelling against your parents, binging on alcohol, self-harming, or eating excessive amounts of food. Whenever you have an urge to do something harmful, it is important to stop everything you are doing, tap into your logical mind, and talk yourself out of performing those actions.

Since strong emotions are temporary, they will naturally subside, and the strong urge you felt will also disappear.

Below are a few questions to ask yourself whenever you sense strong urges.

1. *Describe your urge and give it a rating from 1–5 (1 = weak and 5 = strong).*

_____

_____

_____

_____

_____

_____

2. What events, thoughts, or memories have triggered this urge?

_____

_____

_____

_____

_____

3. What strong emotion is behind this urge?

_____

_____

_____

_____

_____

4. Provide a list of negative consequences for responding to your urge (at least three).

_____

_____

_____

_____

_____

_____

5. Provide a list of positive benefits of controlling your urge (at least three).

_____

_____

_____

_____

6. What are alternative behaviors you can perform, instead of giving into your urge?

_____

_____

_____

_____

7. Who can you reach out to and speak to about your urge? Note: It doesn't need to be a friend or family member.

_____

_____

_____

_____

_____

_____

Now that you have learned how to name, describe, and cope with strong emotions, the following chapter will explore the second goal: How to identify impulsive behaviors.

Chapter 7

> *Never make a permanent decision based on a temporary emotion.*
>
> **-Anonymous**

8 Exercises to Identify Impulsive Behaviors

4 Exercises to Reverse Hyperarousal

Hyperarousal is a state that your body enters when it is feeling stressed. One of the first signs of hyperarousal is an accelerating heart rate. This is often followed by other physical symptoms like shortness of breath, sweaty palms, and feeling disorientated.

During a state of hyperarousal, your main focus is on getting out of danger. Instead

Instead of thinking logically about your next move, you are more likely to act based on impulses. For example, you might say hurtful words, or behave inappropriately, just to regain a sense of control in your body. Emotions like anger, anxiety, and irritability, are common during this state–and the more intense these feelings get, the heightened the arousal becomes.

To get out of a state of hyperarousal, your body needs to return to "normal." In this sense, normal is the feeling of being calm, grounded, and connected to your body. Your logical mind turns back on, and you are able to think clearly about the best way forward. The following exercises will show you how to reverse the state of hyperarousal through relaxation techniques.

Box Breathing

When you are hyperaroused, it is common to experience shortness of breath. Short and irregular breathing contributes to the heightened stress and anxiety, making you stay in the state of hyperarousal for longer.

Breathing exercises can help you deliberately slow down your breathing and get more oxygen into your lungs, which increases the supply of oxygen to the brain. This process stimulates the parasympathetic nervous system and promotes a sense of calmness throughout your body.

Box breathing is a simple breathing exercise that encourages slow and long breaths. The instructions are simple:

😔 Imagine you are tracing a box with each inhale and exhale breath.

😔 Start by inhaling for four counts, drawing the first vertical line of the box.

😔 Hold your breath for four counts, drawing the horizontal line of the box.

😔 Exhale for another four counts, drawing the second vertical line of the box.

😔 Hold your breath for four counts and close the box.

😔 Complete this pattern until you are feeling relaxed.

Grounding Practices

When you are stressed, you are out of touch with your body. Grounding shifts your focus away from your thoughts and emotions, and helps you tap into the present moment and focus on the physical world around you.

When you are grounded, you are able to stop the cycle of negative thinking and reconnect with reality. This can bring about a great sense of relief!

There are different types of grounding practices that you can do around the house, which can bring about a state of calmness. Below are a few suggestions that you can try:

- ☺ Have a cold shower.

- ☺ Suck on a sour piece of candy.

- ☺ Sing along to the lyrics of your favorite song.

- ☺ Squeeze a pillow as tightly as you can.

- ☺ Look around you and find an interesting detail you haven't noticed before.

- ☺ Go for a swim.

- ☺ Notice the weight of your body pressing on a chair.

- ☺ Chew a snack 32 times.

- ☺ Practice a dance routine.

Write down five more grounding practices of your own to add onto the list:

_____

_____

_____

_____

_____

_____

_____

_____

_____

_____

Express Yourself Through Movement

Strong emotions are often stored in your body as pain, discomfort, or tension. By moving your body freely, you can relieve some of this tension, while also reconnecting to yourself.

Go into your safe place (refer to Exercise 8), or somewhere private where you can feel comfortable moving freely. Imagine that you became your emotion, like becoming the fear or anger you feel inside. How would you walk or move your body?

Practice the movements freely and unleash the buildup of tension. If you need music to help you get inspired, play a soundtrack that feels similar to how you feel.

Progressive Muscle Relaxation

Another great exercise to release a buildup of tension in your body is known as progressive muscle relaxation. The objective is to start from your head and work down to your toes, tensing and relaxing every major muscle in your body.

The sensation of tensing and relaxing your muscles creates a calming effect. Below are the instructions to practice this technique:

- Lie down on your bed or flat surface with your legs slightly apart and arms resting by your sides.

- Tighten your facial muscles and hold for a few seconds, then relax your face.

- Rotate your chin to the left and hold for a few seconds, before returning to center. Rotate your chin to the other side and hold once again, then return to center.

- Lift your shoulders as high as you can. Hold for a few seconds, then bring them back down.

- Tighten your fists. Lift your arms toward your shoulders and hold this position for a few seconds, then lower your arms and release your fists.

- Tighten your back muscles by lifting your chest toward the sky and bringing your shoulders inward. Hold the position for a few seconds, then return to normal position.

☺ Tighten your stomach muscles by performing a sit up. Stay up for a few seconds before making your way back down.

☺ Straighten your legs and tighten them as much as you can. Hold this position for a few seconds, then release.

☺ Tense your feet by scrunching them up, and hold for a few seconds. Release the grip and relax.

☺ You have completed the first round! If you would like to complete another round, start at the beginning with your facial muscles.

4 Exercises to Control Impulsive Behaviors

Acting impulsively means taking decisions without thinking clearly about them. Impulsive behaviors can feel satisfying in the short-term because they are performed when you are still running on adrenaline and feeling the 'high' of being in survival mode. However, once your logical mind returns and you get to reflect on your behaviors, you can be filled with regret and embarrassment.

Impulsive behaviors are risky and addictive. Overtime, they can cause you to turn to the wrong kinds of pleasures, like drugs and alcohol, unsafe sex, gambling, or shopping addictions to deal with stress and anxiety. Before causing great harm to yourself and others, it is important to get your impulsive behaviors under control.

The following exercises will show you how!

Record Your Anger Triggers

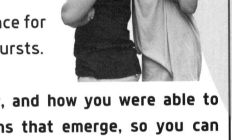

Anger issues refers to uncontrollable anger that is triggered by ordinary life situations. Think of it as being hypersensitive to anything that might cause frustration, even if it is hearing your name called out in a strange way. Identifying and recording your anger triggers can help you plan in advance for certain life situations, and avoid sudden emotional outbursts.

Use the following table to record every anger trigger, and how you were able to control your emotions. Be on the lookout for patterns that emerge, so you can identify your main sources of frustration. The first row has been completed for you.

Date	Situation/trigger	Angry thought	How did you control your emotion?
05/09	I got yelled at by my parents.	"I just wish they would shut up and stop bothering me!"	I practiced a breathing exercise and distracted myself by reading a chapter from a book.

Date	Situation/trigger	Angry thought	How did you control your emotion?

Identifying Suicidal Thoughts and Behaviors

Suicide is the third leading cause of death amongst young people between the ages of 15-24 years, in the US (SAVE, 2020). With such high rates, it is important to not shy away from this topic, or ignore any suicidal thoughts and feelings you may have. The important part when experiencing suicidal thoughts or feelings is to first show yourself compassion and realize how common it is to have these kinds of thoughts and feelings. Secondly, you should work toward controlling the impulse to act on those thoughts and feelings.

Below are a few questions to help you explore what suicidal thoughts and behaviors mean and look like for you.

1. *What are your thoughts on suicide?*

_____

_____

_____

_____

2. Have you ever thought to unalive yourself? Describe what you were going through at the time and how the thought came about.

_____

_____

_____

_____

_____

3. Have you ever spoken to someone about suicide?

_____

_____

_____

_____

_____

_____

4. *Below are examples of different suicidal thoughts. Place a tick next to each thought you have entertained. Notice how some of these thoughts sound like everyday language.*

Suicidal thought	Tick (X)
My life is not worth living.	
My friends and family would be better off without me.	
What's the point of being alive?	
I feel like there is no way out.	
I feel depressed.	
I sleep too much and don't have an appetite.	
I don't care about my hobbies anymore.	

Suicidal thought	Tick (X)
I prefer to isolate myself from everyone.	
I feel worthless.	
I blame myself for the way things are in my life.	
Nobody understands me.	
Nobody loves me.	

5. *The following table shows practical ways that you can manage suicidal thoughts. Go through the table and place a tick next to each coping strategy you have tried. Notice how many different ways you can take action when experiencing suicidal thoughts.*

Coping strategies to manage suicidal thoughts	Tick (X)
Seek professional help immediately.	
Stay consistent with taking medication and following the treatment plan.	
Taking your thoughts seriously and showing concern.	

Coping strategies to manage suicidal thoughts	Tick (X)
Finding a loved one to talk to about your feelings.	
Deliberately being around positive people and avoiding being alone.	
Being open and honest about the pressures you are dealing with in your life.	
Maintaining a sober life and avoiding drugs and alcohol.	
Distancing yourself from negative media (i.e. TV shows, social media pages, podcasts, etc.).	
Setting firm boundaries with toxic people, even if it means creating distance.	

Suicidal thoughts and feelings must be taken seriously. If you notice that you are feeling suicidal, even if it occurs once in a while, reach out to a loved one, or contact the National Suicide Prevention Lifeline immediately (1-800-273-8255).

Managing Impulsive Thoughts

Impulsive behaviors begin as impulsive thoughts. These types of thoughts usually appear as "life or death" statements that force you to make a decision RIGHT NOW. When these thoughts enter your mind, it can feel as though you are given an ultimatum and need to act quickly. This however is not true. The clock is not ticking, and you have all the time in the world to decide the best action to take.

Impulsive thoughts can sound like:

☺ Don't do that!

☺ If you don't act now, you won't...

☺ Don't think about that, focus on this.

☺ Follow my instructions!

☺ Don't trust them!

☺ You better defend yourself!

☺ Don't leave!

☺ Run away right now!

When these thoughts arise in your mind, give yourself a moment to calm down before thinking about taking any action. Once you are calm, break the thought by thinking of the wise thing to do. You can even imagine your grandparents, and how they would respond in that situation.

The following table provides you with examples of impulsive thoughts. Next to each one, provide a wise response to slow down your thinking.

Impulsive thought	Wise response
Don't call them back.	
If you don't say something now, everyone will think you are dumb.	
Don't think about getting in trouble. Just enjoy the pleasure of this moment.	
Do everything I tell you to do.	
Those people can't be trusted.	
If you don't defend yourself and retaliate, you are a coward.	
Don't leave the abusive relationship. Give them another chance!	
Ghost your crush! They aren't who you think they are.	

Checking Your Controlling Behaviors

When things don't go your way, how do you react? Do you accept the outcome and adjust your expectations, or feel angry because your need for control has been triggered?

If you identify as someone who is controlling, part of how you deal with stressful life events is having complete control of your environment. This gives you a sense of safety amidst chaos, and allows you to relax and carry out your routines as normal. When your sense of control is threatened by unexpected situations, you can feel overwhelmed and react emotionally.

Since life is so unpredictable, it is unrealistic to expect things to always go your way, or people to never disappoint you. Instead of desiring complete control over your life, you can increase your stress tolerance levels and give yourself reasons to believe you will overcome every challenge that comes your way!

Answer the following questions about your controlling behaviors.

1. *Think about a controlling behavior you insist upon. For example, you might insist for your friend to call you twice a day, or your parents to fetch you at a specific time from school. Focus on a behavior that carries a 'must' in front of it.*

_____

_____

_____

_____

_____

2. In what ways is this behavior controlling? For example, does it give restrictions, fixed instructions, or extreme expectations of others?

_____

_____

_____

_____

_____

3. What strong emotion is this controlling behavior hiding? What emotion triggers your need to have a sense of control?

_____

_____

_____

_____

_____

4. What are alternative coping strategies to manage this emotion without needing to control others, or your environment?

_____

_____

_____

_____

_____

5. How differently might your life feel if you didn't have to panic about losing control?

_____

_____

_____

_____

_____

6. What positive phrase or mantra can you repeat to yourself to calm down, whenever you sense a lack of control?

_____

_____

_____

_____

_____

Conclusion

It's your reaction to adversity, not adversity itself that determines how your life's story will develop.

-Dieter F. Uchtdorf

Life gets complicated sometimes, especially for modern teenagers whose stress and anxiety rates are comparable to those of adults. Psychotherapy promises teens the kind of support they might not be getting at home or at school. By learning stress management and self-regulation skills, these young people can become better at managing strong emotions, replacing unwanted thoughts, and controlling impulsive behaviors.

This CBT workbook has presented 42 exercises to help your child learn various cognitive behavioral techniques to cope with stress, anxiety, and trauma. Some of the skills that have been reinforced throughout the workbook include:

- ☺ self-awareness

- ☺ cognitive restructuring

- ☺ mindfulness

- ☺ emotional resilience

- ☺ empathy

- ☺ distress tolerance

- ☺ emotional regulation.

The best way to ensure that these skills become part of your child's makeup, is to encourage constant repetition. Use different scenarios or examples to practice the same exercises, over and over again! With time-and patience-your child will develop the assertiveness needed to step out into the world and express who they are!

Dear Reader,

Thank you for choosing to read my workbook. I sincerely hope it has provided you with valuable insights and practical guidance on your personal development journey. Your feedback is incredibly important to me.

If you found this book helpful or thought-provoking, I kindly request that you consider sharing your thoughts through a review. By doing so, you can help others discover the book and make an informed decision about whether it alights with their needs.

Leaving a review is quick and easy. You will just require your smartphone or tablet to scan the QR code below. This will take you to the review page for this workbook, and from there all you have to do is select a star rating, leave an honest review and click submit.

Your review will not only help me grow as an author but will also assist other individuals seeking guidance on their personal development journeys.

I appreciate your time and support. Thank you for being a part of this transformative experience.

Best regards,

Richard Bass.

Richard Bass

Richard Bass is a well-established author with extensive knowledge and background on children's disabilities. He has also experienced first-hand many children and teens who deal with depression and anxiety. Richard also enjoys researching techniques and ideas to better serve students, as well as providing guidance to parents on how to understand and lead their children to success.

Richard wants to share his experience, research, and practices through his writing, as it has proven successful to many parents and students. He feels there is a need for parents and others around the child to fully understand the disability, or mental health of the child. He hopes that with his writing, people will be more understanding of children going through these issues.

In regards to his qualifications, Richard holds a bachelor's and master's degree in education as well as several certifications including Special Education K-12, and Educational Administration. Whenever he is not working, reading, or writing, he likes to travel with his family to learn about different cultures as well as get ideas from all around about the upbringing of children especially those with disabilities. He also researches and learns about different educational systems around the world.

Richard participates in several online groups where parents, educators, doctors, and psychologists share their successes with children with disabilities. He also has his own group where further discussion about his books and techniques take place. Apart from his participation in online groups, Richard also attends training related to the upbringing of students with disabilities and has also led training in this area.

A Message from the Author

If you enjoyed the book and are interested on further updates or just a place to share your thoughts with other readers or myself, please join my Facebook group by scanning below!

If you would be interested on receiving a FREE Planner for kids PDF version, by signing up you will also receive exclusive notifications to when new content is released and will be able to receive it at a promotional price. Scan below to sign up!

Scan below to check out my content on You Tube and learn more about Neurodiversity!

References

American Psychological Association. (2018). Sress in America TM Generation Z. https://www.apa.org/news/press/releases/stress/2018/stress-gen-z.pdf

As One. (2016). Cognitive behavioural therapy (CBT) skills workbook. Hertfordshire Partnership University NHS Foundation Trust.

Bariso, J. (2019, September 30). 28 Emotional intelligence quotes that can help make emotions work for you, instead of against. Incafrica.com. https://incafrica.com/library/justin-bariso-28-emotional-intelligence-quotes-that-can-help-make-emotions-work-for-you-instead-of-against-you

BrainyQuote. (n.d.). Teen quotes. BrainyQuote. Retrieved November 3, 2022, from https://www.brainyquote.com/topics/teen-quotes

Branch, R., & Willson, R. (2012). Cognitive behavioural therapy workbook for dummies, 2nd ed. John Wiley & Sons.

Cleveland Clinic. (2022, April 8). Cognitive behavioral therapy (CBT). Cleveland Clinic. https://my.clevelandclinic.org/health/treatments/21208-cognitive-behavioral-therapy-cbt

Dennish, A. (2018, June 2). "Time to shift." Anne Dennish. https://annedennish.com/2018/06/02/time-to-shift/

Erieau, C. (2019, February 20). The 50 best resilience quotes. Driven App. https://home.hellodriven.com/articles/the-50-best-resilience-quotes/

Fryer, D. (2015, October 15). Ten quotes that sum up CBT perfectly. Daniel Fryer. https://www.danielfryer.com/2015/10/15/ten-quotes-that-sum-up-cbt-perfectly/

Good Reads. (n.d.). Hector Garcia Puigcerver quote. Www.goodreads.com. https://www.goodreads.com/author/show/7033810.Hector_Garcia_Puigcerver

Hanks, J. (2014). Feelings word list: Free download. Wasatch Family Therapy. https://wasatchfamilytherapy.com/blog/archives/27325

Lockett, E. (2022, April 18). *Can you be your own therapist? Why self-therapy may be for you.* Psych Central. https://psychcentral.com/health/self-therapy

Making the Connection. (n.d.). *Positive change through cognitive behavioral therapy.* www.maketheconnection.net. https://www.maketheconnection.net/read-stories/cbt/

Mandic, T. (2019). The PTSD workbook. Between Sessions Resources.

Morin, A. (2020, December 15). Why you should bring your teen to therapy. Verywell Mind. https://www.verywellmind.com/top-reasons-teens-go-to-therapy-2609138

Morin, A. (2022, February 25). Which types of therapy are best for teens? Verywell Mind. https://www.verywellmind.com/therapy-for-teens-2610410

Pietrangelo, A. (2019, December 12). CBT techniques: Tools for cognitive behavioral therapy. Healthline. https://www.healthline.com/health/cbt-techniques#types-of-cbt-techniques

Sacchetti, P. (2018, September 17). How CBT impacts our brain. Collaborative CBT. https://collaborativecbt.com/how-cbt-impacts-our-brain/#:-:text=How%20Does%20CBT%20Physically%20Change

SAVE. (2020). Suicide statistics and facts. SAVE. https://save.org/about-suicide/suicide-statistics/#:-:text=There%20is%20one%20suicide%20death

Schwartz, T. (2015, April 3). The importance of naming your emotions. The New York Times. https://www.nytimes.com/2015/04/04/business/dealbook/the-importance-of-naming-your-emotions.html#:-:text=Noticing%20and%20naming%20emotions%20gives

Smith, K. (2020, November 24). 6 Common triggers of teen stress. Psycom.net. https://www.psycom.net/common-triggers-teen-stress

Washington Post. (2013, January 4). We are meant to forget. Tampa Bay Times. https://www.tampabay.com/news/perspective/we-are-meant--to-forget/1268960/

Whalley, M., & Kaur, H. (2021). What is cognitive behavioral therapy (CBT)? Psychology Tools. https://www.psychologytools.com/self-help/what-is-cbt/

Image References

Cameron, J. M. (2020a). Photo of girl using black smartphone [Online Image]. In Pexels. https://www.pexels.com/photo/photo-of-girl-using-black-smartphone-4144288/

Cameron, J. M. (2020b). Boy in yellow crew neck t shirt wearing white and black vr goggles [Online Image]. In Pexels. https://www.pexels.com/photo/boy-in-yellow-crew-neck-t-shirt-wearing-white-and-black-vr-goggles-4144146/

Fischer, M. (2020). A young student in a classroom [Online Image]. In Pexels. https://www.pexels.com/photo/a-young-student-in-a-classroom-5211478/

Grabowska, K. (2020). Girl in headphones using a phone [Online Image]. In Pexels. https://www.pexels.com/photo/girl-in-headphones-using-a-phone-6256002/

Grabowska, K. (2021a). Girls using a pink laptop [Online Image]. In Pexels. https://www.pexels.com/photo/girls-using-a-pink-laptop-8003527/

Mart Production. (2021). A young man doing his homework while sitting on a bed [Online Image]. In Pexels. https://www.pexels.com/photo/a-young-man-doing-his-homework-while-sitting-on-a-bed-8472957/

Piacquadio, A. (2020). Jolly woman in yellow polo shirt [Online Image]. In Pexels. https://www.pexels.com/photo/jolly-woman-in-yellow-polo-shirt-3785551/

Plavalaguna, D. (2020). Multiracial people with hands raised [Online Image]. In Pexels. https://www.pexels.com/photo/multiracial-people-with-hands-raised-6150584/

Shekhovtcova, A. (2021). Girl in blue white and red plaid shirt lying on bed [Online Image]. In Pexels. https://www.pexels.com/photo/girl-in-blue-white-and-red-plaid-shirt-lying-on-bed-6995747/